howto marketing

series of business self-help books written by practitioners

the little cook book of project management

by Thom Poole

written by Thomas F Poole © 2011 Thom Poole

first published by Lulu in 2011

ISBN: 978-1-4477-6477-9

for Sue
for your support in project managing me!

contents

the little cook book of project management

what is *project management*?

> plans are only good intentions unless they immediately degenerate into hard work.

Peter Drucker

plan to win

there are rules, processes and tools for *project* planning and *project management*.   *project management* skills are not important for project managers alone.

a 'task' does not have to be called a *'project'* in order for *project management* methods to be very useful in its planning and implementation.   even the smallest task can benefit well-chosen *project management* techniques, especially in the planning stage.

any task that requires some preparation to achieve a successful outcome, will probably be done better by using a few *project management* methods.

project management is mainly associated with planning and managing change in an organisation, but a project can exist outside a business.   its methods and tools can be useful far wider than people assume.

project management techniques and planning tools are useful for any tasks in which different outcomes are possible;   where risks of problems and failures exist - and thus need planning and assessing options, and organising activities and resources to deliver the desired result/s.

projects can be any sizes and shape, from small and straightforward to extremely large and highly complex.

examples of *projects* can cover:

- people, staffing and management;
- products and services;
- materials, manufacturing and production;
- IT and communications;
- plant, vehicles, equipment;
- storage, distribution, logistics;
- buildings and premises;
- finance, administration, acquisition and divestment;
- purchasing;
- sales, selling, marketing;
- human resources development and training;
- customer service and relations;
- quality, health and safety;
- legal and professional;
- technical, scientific, research and development;
- new business development;
- and anything else which needs planning and managing within organisations.

source: *www.businessballs.com*

the little cook book of project management

why projects *fail*

unfortunately, many *projects* fail – especially information systems *projects*, failing to delivery against your objectives, timetable or budget. most *projects* fail because they are poorly managed, poorly planned or badly controlled.

common issues include:

not delivering what the user/customer wanted – planning involves understanding what the user/customer actually wants. this is not always what they articulate, so a good *project manager* can read between the lines.

designing to the wrong budget – over developing will either mean that the *project* ends up over budget, or having to skimp on essentials later on. alternatively, under developing from the outset may leave money in the *project* pot, but users unsatisfied

overrunning on deadlines – time is money; so bad time management costs money. in poorly managed *projects*, time slippages cause problems and lead to *project* failure.

over developed '*project*' – in technical *projects*, especially where the user/customer cannot articulate their requirements, technical developers may develop what they want to.

users change their mind – not common in well run projects, but if a long *project* overruns, scope creep can kill a *project*.

common reasons for failure

the list is not exhaustive, but include:

- poor *project* specification

- unrealistic timescales

- timescales that are too long

- inappropriate team members

- insufficient involvement by senior management or sponsorship

- failure to manage user expectations

- failure to manage the changes requires

project management *cycle*

failing to plan is planning to fail

planning is important to ensure everything that needs to be done is completed, and you will achieve your objectives.

the *project management* cycle, below, should be applied, and your findings at each stage noted so that you can identify convergence and keep the *project* in perspective.

the cycle is explained in more detail in the 'ingredients' section of this book.

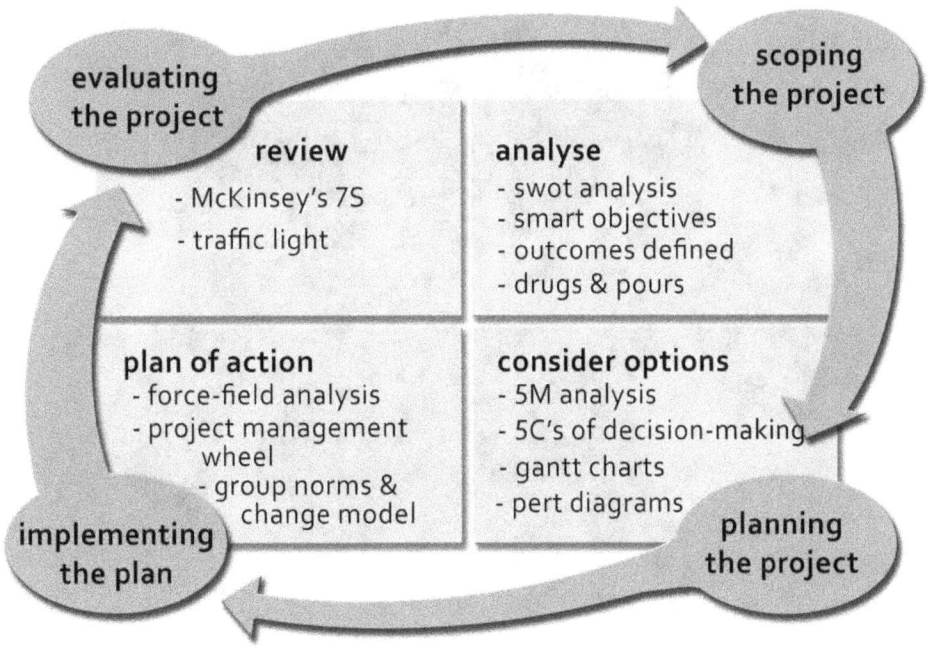

the *project management* cycle
source: the project management pocketbook. Posner, K & Applegarth, M

the little cook book of project management

key roles in *project management*

> " of all the things I've done, the most vital is coordinating the talents of those who work for us and pointing them towards a certain goal. "
>
> *Walt Disney*

key roles

in any *project* you must assemble the right team to deliver a successful result. it is unlikely that you will have a full team at all times.

project sponsor

successful *projects* are normally those that are given direction and support from high-level sponsors within the organisation. it is important that the senior management are ultimately responsible for the *project*.

in many cases, companies will have a *project* board with a spectrum of experts and stakeholders. in PRINCE2 methodology the person is the '*project* executive'.

the sponsor must have sufficient authority in all parts of the organisation impacted by the *project*.

project manager

the *project* manager is responsible for the day-to-day management of the *project*. they would be involved in defining the *project* and ensuring that it is delivered on time, to budget and to the required quality.

the manager also agree, manage and monitor against the *project* plan, allocating and utilising resources in an efficient manner and maintaining a co-operative, motivated and successful team.

source: JISC infoNet

the project *board*

usually comprising of:

- a chair who may also be the *project* sponsor.

- a senior user to represent all future users of the result of the *project*.

- a senior supplier to represent the sections of the organisation and any external suppliers, whose work will assist in the outcome of the *project*.

- a 'customer' or customer champion, representing the stakeholders who will benefit from the result of the *project*.

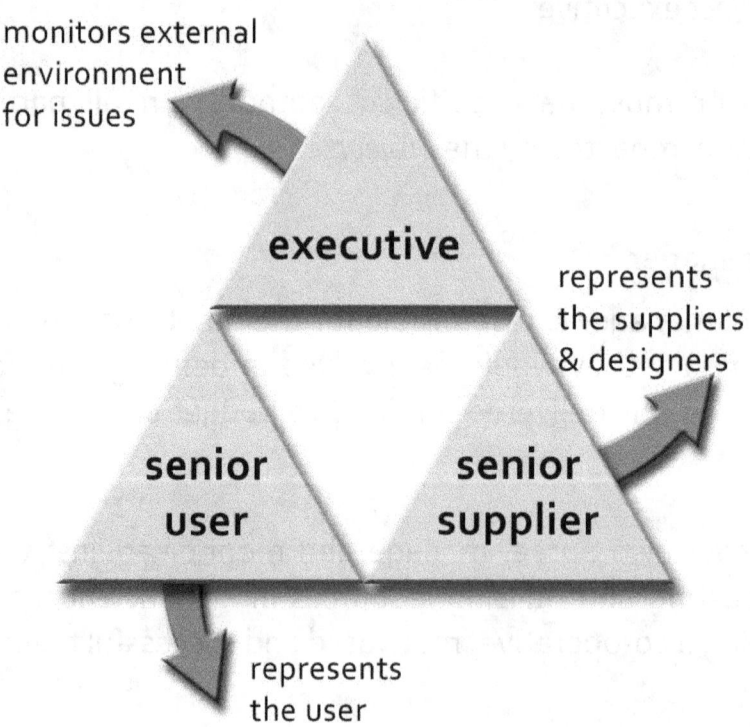

monitors external
environment
for issues

executive

represents
the suppliers
& designers

**senior
user**

**senior
supplier**

represents
the user

thom poole

the executive

normally a senior manager from the organisation, the executive has ultimate responsibility for the *project* and 'owns' the business case throughout the life of the *project*.   he or she has the following specific responsibilities:

- oversee the development of the *project* brief and business case.

- authorise expenditure levels, set milestone tolerances and ensure funding is available.

- authorise or reject proposed changes to cost or timescale beyond tolerance levels and all proposed changes to scope, checking for possible effects on the business case – guarding against scope creep.

- ensure risks and issues are being tracked and mitigated/ resolved.

- liaise/report to programme or corporate management on progress

- organise and chair meetings of the *project* board.

- authorise the *project's* continuance or early closure at stage review meetings of the *project* board.

- authorise formal closure of the *project*.

- conduct post-*project* reviews to ensure benefits are realised.

the little cook book of project management

the senior user

the senior user represents the users on the *project* board.   if there is a user group, this person will often chair it.   the senior user's specific duties are as outlined:

- ensure that the desired outcome of the *project* is specified.

- co-ordinate the agreement of users of a set of acceptance criteria containing measurable and tangible descriptors.

- organise and chair meetings of the *project* user group.

- organise and monitor user testing of *project* outputs, ensuring that any issues arising are adequately recorded and communicated.

- monitor the *project's* progress from a user requirements point of view.

- manage two-way communications with the users.

- resolve any issues or conflicts including conflicts of priorities of users.

- monitor and manage user-related risks.

the little cook book of project management

the senior supplier

the senior supplier is responsible for the quality of the *project* – inputs and outputs. where multiple external suppliers are involved, there may be more than one person in this role.   specific responsibilities include:

- approval of supplier specifications - this may be by approving product descriptions or specifications.

- ensure that supplier resources are made available for *project* work.

- resolve any supplier conflicts.

- advise the *project* on design and development strategies.

- monitor potential changes for impact on the quality of products from suppliers.

- monitor and manage risks from a supplier viewpoint.

- ensure adequate quality control procedures are adhered to by suppliers.

source: JISC infoNet

the little cook book of project management

ingredients of *project management?*

"my personal philosophy is not to undertake a *project* unless it is manifestly important and nearly impossible.

Edwin Land
poloroid camera inventor

scoping the project

setting objectives

collect facts, information, opinions and needs.   question assumptions and define what is in and what can be excluded.

swot analysis

determine the strengths (**S**) and weaknesses (**W**) of the *project* in terms of the 'internal' situation.   the opportunities (**O**) and threats (**T**) of the *project* in terms of external or potential situation.

define outcomes and resources

> scoping the *project* to understand its complexity and the range of activities required to complete the *project*. the factors to be considered include: time, cost, quality and quantity – and the mix thereof.

setting objectives

> based on the outcomes, how would you measure the results? by using smart objectives:
>
> > **specific** – is the activity to which the objective relates clearly and specifically defined?
> >
> > **measurable** – will the outcomes sought be visible when the *project* task is completed?
> >
> > **achievable** – is the entire task physically possible, and objectives achievable?
> >
> > **rewarding** – how will the *project* benefit the organisation, team or individual?
> >
> > **time-bound** – what is the deadline for the *project*, or milestones?

the little cook book of project management

sponsors 'drugs' test

to evaluate the channels of influence in the *project*, apply the 'drugs' test:

decider – authorises and initiates *project* and agrees the terms of reference.

recommender – wants changes and needs to be convinced it is an integral part of the business.   *projects* will always have supporters and detractors – make sure this person stays on your side!

user – implements and influences recommenders.

gatekeeper – experts who influence the decider and can block access to deciders and recommenders.   these people do not necessarily have official positions.

stakeholders – can be outside of the *project* team/board.

source: the project management pocketbook. Posner, K & Applegarth, M

communications

information gathering is a key requirement in *project management*, and must start prior to the start of the *project*.   one method for information gathering is 'pour'.

1. **plan** - what to tell and ask.

2. **outline** your understanding – clarify objectives and seek constant feedback.

3. **use** open questions – why, where, who, when, what and how!

4. **reflect** – use closed question for confirmation.

5. **summarise** – agree actions.

planning the project

consider your options by using the 5C's of decision-making to guide the implementation

consider

- clarify the nature of the *project*, time and other constraints.
- ask what information you need.
- identify objectives.

consult

- gather the maximum amount of information available.
- call meetings of those involved.
- brainstorm where necessary.
- decide at which point the consultation will stop.

crunch

- review all the options and take decisions.
- write down your implementation plan.

communicate

- provide briefings on what will happen, why and who the decisions affect.
- back-up briefings with written confirmations.
- make sure everyone understands when the decision will be implemented.

check

- check that the briefing is carried out.
- run spot checks to monitor effectiveness.
- review the impact of the decision and take corrective action.

the little cook book of project management

5M analysis

we operate better when *projects* are broken into 'bitesized' chunks. one way to facilitate the planning is using the 5M framework:

machinery

manpower

materials

methods

money

use this framework against all elements or obstacles.

gantt charts

there are few resources more synonymous with *project management* than gantt charts.   it is probably one of the easiest tools to understand and use, and yet can be one of the most comprehensive.

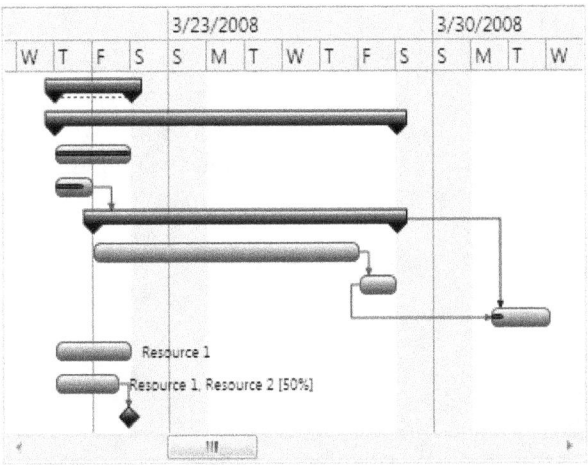

pert diagrams

pert stands for **p**rogramme **e**valuation and **r**eview **t**echnique and is a more sophisticated tool than gantt charts. events are represented by circles and activities by connecting arrows.

pert diagrams are most useful in identifying critical paths in *projects*, in terms of best-case or worst-case timings. computer programmes such as the popular MS *Project* allow the user to switch between a gantt and pert format to display and manager their *project*.

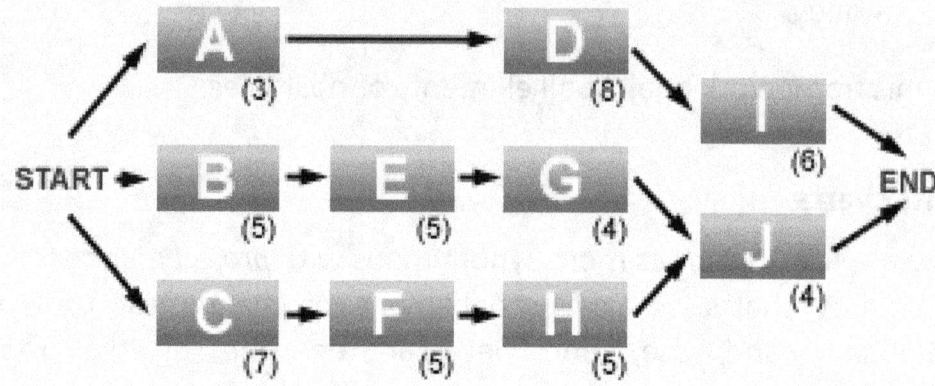

implementing the plan

planning is vital for any *project*, but to get the plan to work it must be implanted.   the trick is to keep as close to the original plan as possible.

force-field analysis

this tool is probably the most politically sensitive because it looks critically at the business. graphically, you use the size of the arrows of 'force' to indicate the weighting you give to that issue.

some issues (arrows) cancel each other out, others provide an element of balance.

positive forces

> these are driving forces in your business that favour change. the positive forces are normally displayed on the left.

negative forces

> restraining forces the resist change. normally displayed on the right.

project management wheel

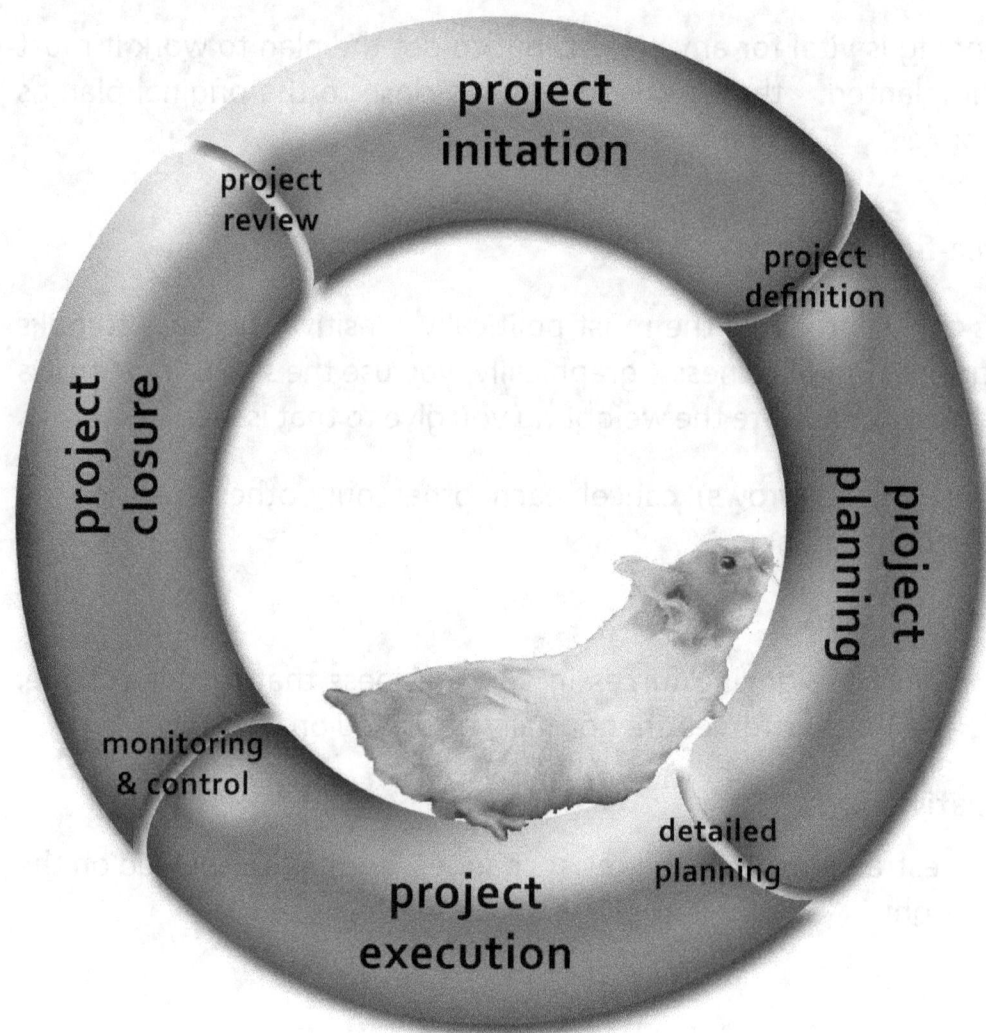

the little cook book of project management

team dynamics

when implementing the plan, team work is vital. committee decisions can stifle innovation, but projects are more likely to fail if decisions are not shared.

in team work, **risk** is the 'father of innovation':

relationships within the team

information shared between team members

support from the *project* leader

kindness to listen to the ideas of others

when doing this, a trust building method is to keep communications visible for the whole team. keeping information secret and hidden from some members of the team can only lead to resentment. each member of the team should be responsible for implementing the part of the *project* they are charged to do, and this includes communicating it with others.

feedback

giving and receiving feedback is important in teamwork, and a useful process is the '*helper*' method:

hear each member's contribution

elaborate with additional positive examples

look at all members' idea for improvement

promote additional suggestions for improvement

empower the team: don't dictate

recognise overall positive behaviours, results and contributions

group norms

it is said that all groups follow four stages of development.   along with an understanding of personality traits, tools such as Belbin can help you match roles and characters:

forming

the group must first get together and gel within the framework of the *project*, its objectives and constraints.

storming

after formation, all aims and objectives of the *project* should be questioned and conflicting views addressed openly.

norming

because of the possible conflicts - policy and procedures should be drawn up and agreed by group consensus.   a good *project* manager should be aware of possible issues between team members from this point on.

performing

the group should adhere to the policy and procedures and works effectively towards the *project* objectives.

evaluating the project

evaluation begins during the *project*, ironing out any issues that arise. novice *project* managers should probably start evaluating their projects and their own contributions from the start, using the tools outlined herein.

McKinsey 7S tool

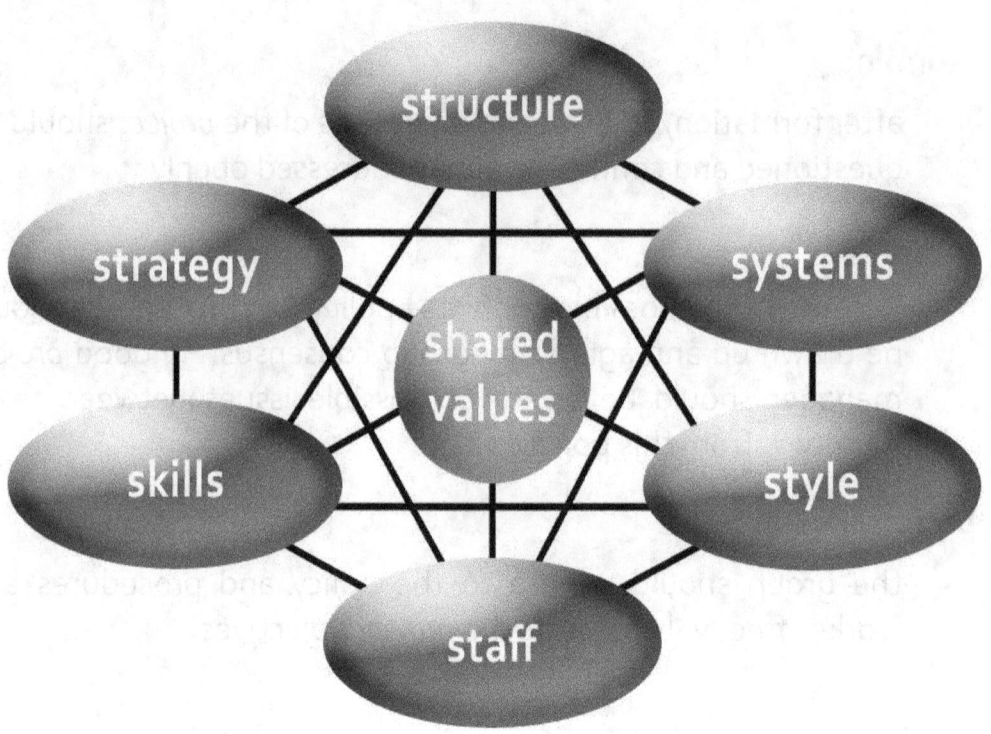

the McKinsey 7S model

the little cook book of project management

this model can be used in the planning and evaluation stage.   it comprises of:

strategy – the vision and business plan

systems – manual and computer processes

staff – the affected members and how they integrate

skills – future knowledge and skills training

style – methods of communication

shared values – culture and ethos of the business, brand and people

structure – reporting lines and framework

traffic lights

traffic lights are a questioning technique:

- what went well in the *project*?

- what didn't go that well?

- what could be changed for the next project?

- what was missing, or missed but not foreseen?

For each element of the *project*, it is possible to assign a 'traffic-light' colour:

red: what should we stop doing?

amber: what do we need to consider continuing, changing or stopping?

green: what did we do well that should be imparted to other *project* teams?

the little cook book of project management

the little cook book of project management

project management recipes

> "nothing is more difficult, and therefore more precious, than being able to decide.
>
> *Napoleon Bonaparte*

simplified project management *process*

there are many different 'processes' in *project management*, but they all adhere to a similar basic methodology.

the simplified process is:

- **assemble team** – assemble, or define the *project* planning and development teams. define roles and responsibilities.

- **define *project* objective/s** – the *project* team should agree the overall purpose of the *project* and the detailed objectives, including all milestones.

- **define *project* scope** – using a work breakdown structure (wbs), the *project* scope is agreed and communicated.

- **construct an initial plan** – taking the tasks in the wbs, the *project manager* builds the project plan, timelines, budgets and critical path.

- **add resources, costs and risks, etc** – working with the *project* staff, the project manager estimates all resources, cash-flows.

- **obtain stakeholder buy-in** – to ensure that the *project* meets the objectives of the stakeholders, they must be involved throughout the process.

- **publish the plan** – when the plans are well communicated, the team pulls together to the common goal.

- **collect progress information** – the *project* manager must collect all the information and communicate it amongst the team.

- **analyse current status** – keep up to date with the progress of the *project* – sticking points and successes.

- **adjust the plan and manage any changes** – changes should be kept to a minimum, but everything should be documented, agreed and communicated.

- **close *project*** – the *project* team must close the *project*, irrespective of the conclusion. learn lessons from the *project* and document them for future *projects*.

the little cook book of project management

waterfall model

the waterfall model is a sequential design process when each stage follows the previous one. it is an over simplified methodology that can provide great flexibility.

the danger with a sequential model is that scope creep can often continuously delay the *project*, but is easier to manage from the perspective of the *project manager*.

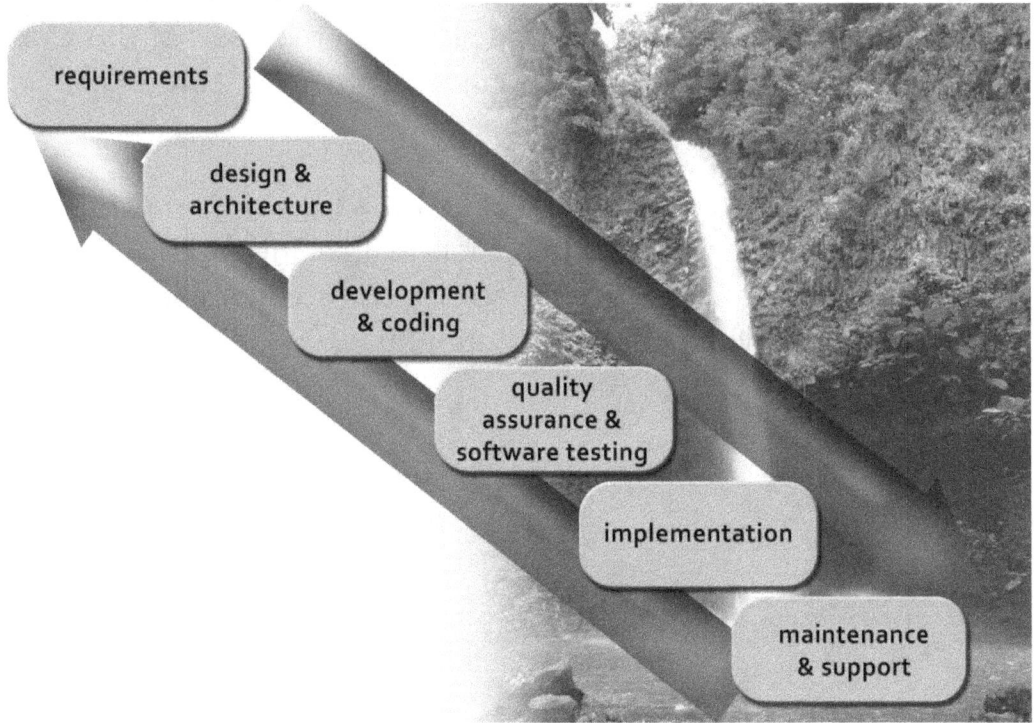

prince2

prince2 is a structured approach to *project management,* developed in 1996 as a generic *project management* method.   it provides a method for managing *projects* within a clearly defined framework. **prince2** describes procedures to coordinate people and activities in a *project,* how to design and supervise the *project,* and what to do if the *project* has to be adjusted if it does not develop as planned.

each process is specified with its key inputs and outputs and with specific goals and activities to be carried out.   this allows automatic control of any deviations from the plan.   on the basis of this close monitoring, the *project* can be undertaken in a controlled and organised way.

prince2 provides a common language for all team members.   the various management roles and responsibilities involved in a *project* are fully described and are adaptable to suit the complexity of the *project* and skills within the organisation.

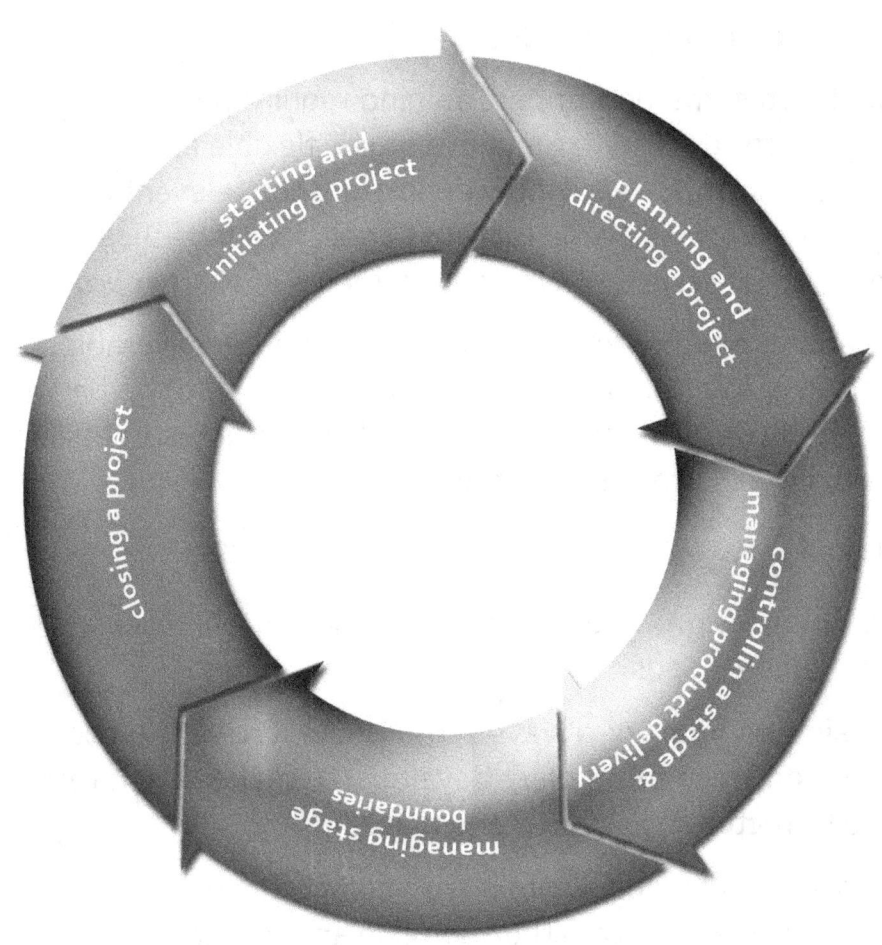

prince2 cycle

agile project management

this is an iterative method of determining requirements, mainly for software *projects*, delivering them in a highly flexible and interactive manner. it sets empowered individuals from the relevant business, with supplier and customer input at its core. agile techniques are best used in small-scale *projects* or on elements of a larger *project*.

it is a variant of an iterative life cycle where deliverables are submitted in stages or milestones. one big difference between agile and iterative development is that delivery times in agile are often given in weeks rather than months.

core rules of agile

- **simple design:** use the simplest design that solves your immediate needs

- **design as you go:** always scrub and exercise the code you work on while the project develops, to make sure it remains well structured, designed and written.

- **incremental steps:** when changing or adding code, take the smallest step you can, then compile and test again.

- **independent steps:** don't mix up the things you do - when you fix a bug, fix the bug, when you add a feature, add the feature.

- **know and use your tools with purpose:** especially for tasks beyond writing code - like design and documentation, know the available tools, use those that help you, and always understand why you do what you do.

- **the meta rule:** use only the principles and techniques that actually work for you.

the little cook book of project management

advantages of agile

- you can react much more flexible to requirement changes and additions.

- the overall design remain simple almost "by itself".

- by scrubbing the code you're working on, the most important parts get most attention, and you don't invest extra time into changing what doesn't need to be changed.

- when cleaning up your code is technically part of the development process, you have much better chances to end up with a well commented and documented orthogonal readable code base.

- you might be able to start coding earlier (although you won't necessarily be faster overall).

- you won't end up in the dead ends.

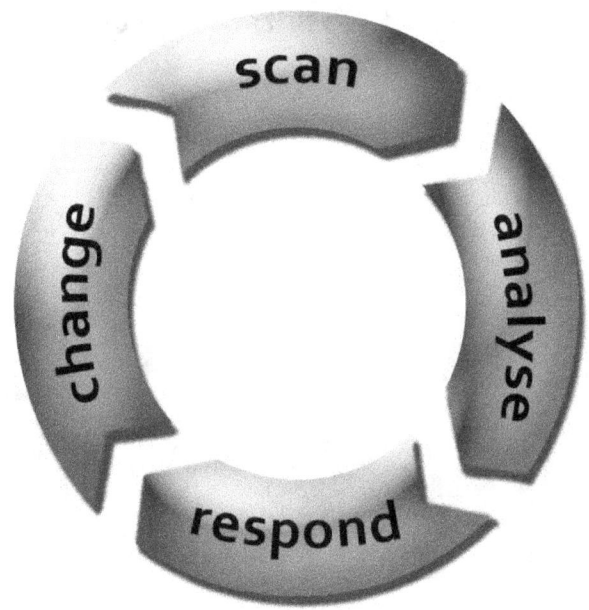

hermes methodology

hermes is a software development method using phases. developed by the Swiss government, this method uses a system that allows phases to be repeated as required.   having been developed by federal funds, it is mandatory for all national *projects* in Switzerland.

a danger of this 'repetitive' element of phases is that scope creep can delay *projects* – just look at many software *projects*.

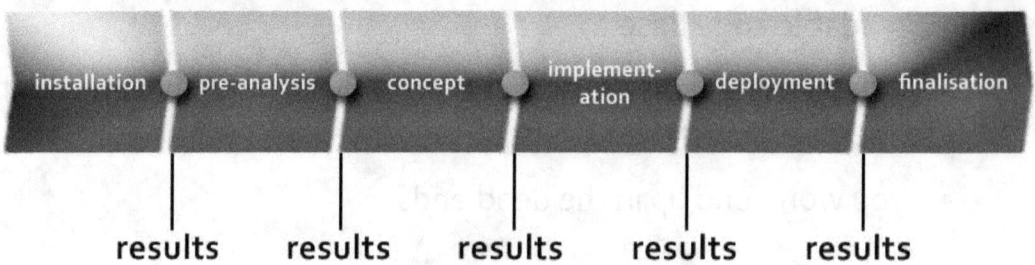

dsdm methodology

dynamic systems development method or dsdm is a *project management* standard based on agile. it is an organised, common-sense process focused on delivering business solutions quickly and efficiently.

dsdm focuses on delivery rather than just team activities, and makes heavy use of prototyping so that all stakeholders have a clear picture of all aspects of the system.

why use dsdm?

- results of development are directly and immediately visible.

- since the users are actively involved in the development of the system, they are more likely to embrace it and take it on.

- basic functionality is delivered quickly, it can be delivered at regular intervals.

- eliminates bureaucracy and breaks down the communication barrier between interested parties.

- because of constant feedback from the users, the system being developed is more likely to meet the need it was commissioned for.

- early indicators of whether *project* will work or not, rather than a nasty surprise halfway through the development

- system is delivered on time and on budget.

- ability of the users to affect the *project's* direction.

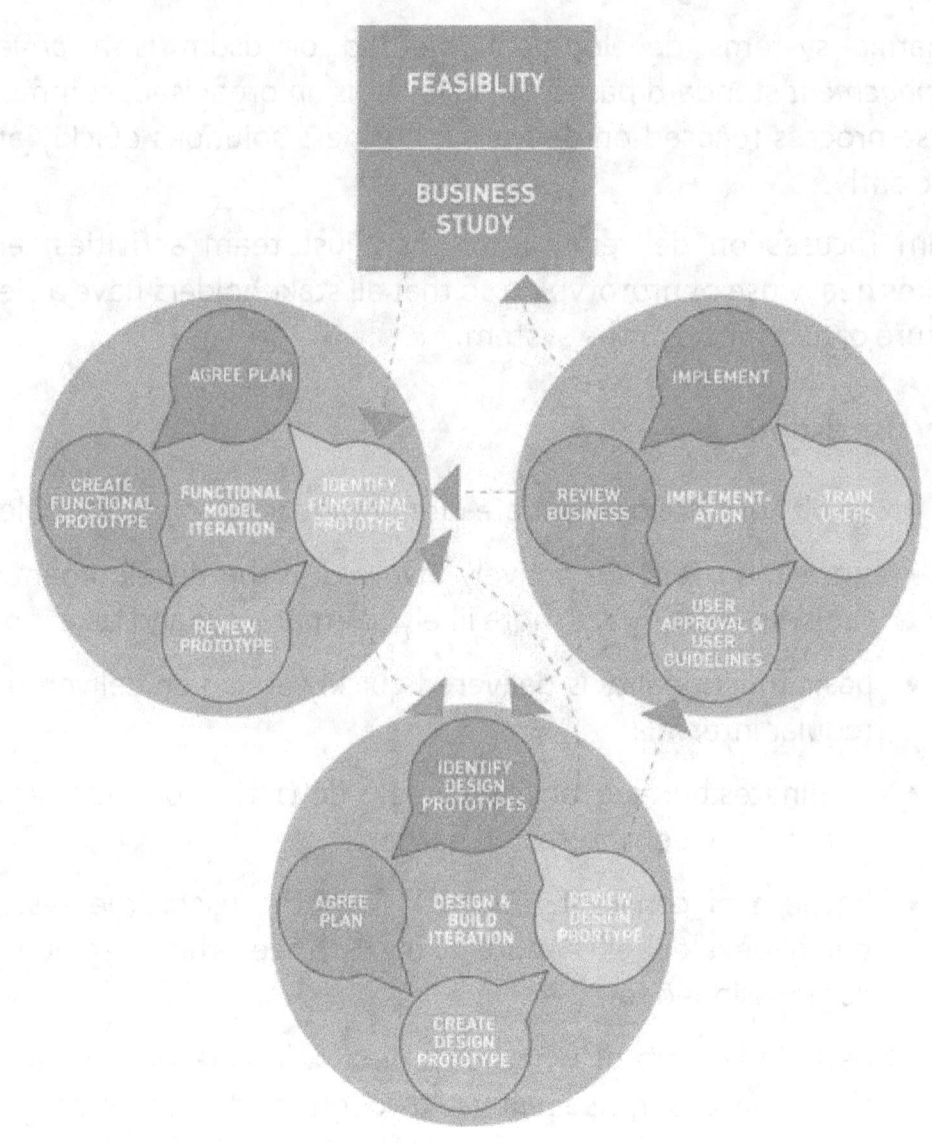

dsdm methodology

project *failure statistics*

- **51% erp** implementations were unsuccessful (source: Robbins-Gioia survey)

- only **34% of executives** were satisfied with *project* implementations (source: Conference Board survey)

- over **61% of it *projects*** failed in Canada (source: KPMG Canada survey)

- **31.1% of *projects* were cancelled** before they even got completed, a further **52.7% of *projects* cost 189%** of their original estimates (source: the Chaos report)

- **7 out of 10 it *projects* 'fail'** in some respect (source: OASIG study)

conclusion

"operations keeps the lights on, strategy provides a light at the end of the tunnel, but *project management* is the train engine that moves the organisation forward.

Joy Gumz

project management is the management of an organisation's future. a good *project manager* will instinctively use a tried and tested methodology to deliver the results.

using a recognised *project management* technique allows new team members to integrate with a *project* faster than using a bespoke system. all processes will have failings, but the best fit will produce the best results.

the author is not a fan of *projects* in which time and/or specifications can be freely adjusted. in my experience a good *project* is properly planned and scoped, the specifications and designs frozen at appropriate points in the process. software development uses *project management* most frequently with flexible elements such as deadlines and specifications.

"one characteristic of winners is they always look upon
themselves as a do it yourself *project*.

Denis Waitley

about the author

Thom Poole is a professional chartered marketer who has spent his career in developing customer-centric products and services.

during the course of writing his dissertation for his marketing masters, Thom identified trust as being a key factor in business success, forming the basis of his first book 'Play It By Trust'.

with a long relationship with *project management*, Thom has worked for some of the most innovative global companies, as an employee and consultant.

a professor of marketing at Grenoble, Thom has also created the first MSc in digital marketing, being delivered by a London business school.

this book was written to provide a quick guide to helping individuals and businesses understand the elements, impact and benefits of marketing.

understanding and quantifying marketing and *project* marketing is an ongoing task, and this book is only one step on the journey.

for more information, please visit Thom's websites:

www.jack-marketing.com

www.about-marketing.co.uk

other titles in the howto marketing series:

Principles of Marketing	Product Marketing
Price Marketing	Promotional Marketing
e-Promotional Marketing	Web Marketing
NPD Marketing	International Marketing
Marketing Planning	Marketing Audits
Customer Relationship Marketing	Mobile Marketing
Web Design for the Terrified	Direct Marketing
Search Engine Marketing	The Little Cook Book of Trust
The Little Cook Book of Marketing	
The Little Cook Book of Social Media Marketing	

www.ingramcontent.com/pod-product-compliance
Lightning Source LLC
Chambersburg PA
CBHW081221170526
45165CB00009B/2903